Why Pray When You Can Take Pills and Worry?

D1220462

Why PRAY When You Can Take Pills and Worry?

One Frazzled Mother's Guide for Raising Teens

PATRICIA WILSON

UPPER
ROOM BOOKS
NASHVILLE

Why Pray When You Can Take Pills and Worry?

Copyright © 1994 Patricia Wilson.
 All rights reserved.

No part of this book may be reproduced in any manner whatsoever without written permission of the publisher except in
brief quotations embodied in critical articles or reviews. For
information address The Upper Room, 1908 Grand Avenue,
P.O. Box 189, Nashville, Tennessee 37202-0189.

Unless otherwise indicated scripture quotations are from
The New Revised Standard Version of the Bible, copyright
© 1989 by the Division of Christian Education of the National
Council of the Churches of Christ in the United States of
America. Used by permission.

Scripture quotations designated NIV are from the *Holy Bible,
New International Version.* Copyright © 1973, 1978, 1984
International Bible Society. Used by permission of Zondervan
Bible Publishers.

Cover Design: Susan Scruggs
First Printing: May 1994 (7)
Library of Congress Catalog Card Number: 93-61042
ISBN: 0-8358-0694-4

Printed in the United States of America

For the Woods who had one,
For the St. Onges who had two,
For the Eastons who had three,
And for the Armstrongs who had four

Contents

Introduction

My mother always told me that if I wanted to do something badly enough and if there was a book about it in the library, I could do it. As a result of this sterling advice, I am a "self-help book" junkie. I'll buy a self-help book on anything from _How to Lose Thirty Pounds in Thirty Days_ (and gain it back in ten) to _How to Play the Piano without Memorizing a Note_ to _How to Find a Fortune in Garage Sales_. I've also dabbled in _Kitchen Wiring Made Easy_, _A Hundred Uses for Egg Cartons,_ and _The Dog Owner's Guide_. When I became a proud mother, I attacked the problem with my usual method. I looked for a book in the library that told me "how to." There was no shortage of such books. Starting with Dr. Spock, I moved confidently up through the years, surviving the "terrible twos" and the "fearless fours," coping with everything from chicken pox to visits to the dentist. From there, parenting was a snap as expert after expert imparted priceless advice on how to cultivate and nurture the little lives in my care.

Then, something happened. My children became teenagers. The good advice, the infallible guidelines, the step-by-step instructions, the knowledge, and the expert techniques failed! Desperately, I searched bookstores, libraries, friends' bookshelves, even flea markets, looking for the golden sources of information that had taught me everything from how to reupholster a couch to how to find my inner child. None of them could teach me how to raise teenagers. It wasn't as if I didn't give all parenting techniques a whirl. I tried being tough, caring, empathetic, militant, open, aloof, relaxed, strict, gentle, dictatorial, autocratic, democratic, and bureaucratic. I even tried being *fun*! Nothing worked.

My children are no longer teenagers. I have survived. I think they survived too. Now is a good time to tell you about some of the adventures we've had on the bumpy road from adolescence to adulthood. Some of the adventures have been exciting, even exhilarating. Others have been tough traveling. Perhaps my telling both the good and the bad (and even the ugly) of living with, growing with, and coping with teenagers will give you the courage to carry on. If nothing else, I hope that my journey will make yours a little easier.

1.

The Kiss-off Dinner

The Beatitudes
(Matthew 5:1-12)

One

☺ _I called it the "kiss-off dinner." I suppose someone with a more romantic frame of mind might have called it a "rite of passage."_

I made reservations at our local classy restaurant and invited Nathan's current girlfriend and Cherith's boyfriend to join the family for dinner. Nate was heading off to college; Cherith had already left for her college; and Marnella had finally found a job and an apartment she could call her own. One way or another, their individual destinies were taking them out of the nest and into the big wide world. The "nest" they were leaving was mine. It was time to kiss them good-bye.

A farewell supper seemed a good way to do it. As I looked around the table, I considered how far we had all come together. There was my mother who had often acted as a surrogate parent to Nathan and Cherith while I was surviving the agonies of single-parenthood. Gerald, husband number two, who had taken on my entire menagerie (two kids, three cats, two donkeys, seventeen chickens, and one dog), and who had added his own daughter to the mix, had survived eight years with all of us. Nathan, now an entertaining young man, was far removed from the fearful child who had firmly tied himself to my apron strings. Beautiful Cherith, tall, graceful, and perfectly groomed, was equally far removed from the ugly duckling who had stuck out like a sore thumb amidst the little swans in her ballet class. Marnella, a latecomer to the family circle, had decided to try her wings by coming to the wilds of the country to live with us. Now, two years later, she was ready to take another leap— from this safe nest to a life of her own. And me? Well, I was a little older, a little rounder, and definitely a little wiser than the woman who had embarked on this journey.

We had all changed, grown, matured, and mellowed! It hadn't always been easy. At any given moment, someone wasn't speaking to someone else. With the cataclysmic ups and downs of the teenage temperament, the atmosphere had often felt as if we were living on the brink of an active volcano. Yet, we could all sit around the table and laugh and joke comfortably with one another. I suppose that fact alone made it all worth while.

As dinner progressed, small vignettes of reality reminded me that we were a long way from the perfect family of "Leave It to Beaver" and "Father Knows Best." Marnella fussily ordered her vegetarian dinner. (Have you ever tried feeding a vegetarian teenager?) Nathan told Cherith she had on too much makeup (always a good way to add a little zest to the moment). Cherith retaliated with a few choice words. (Where does she pick them up? I wonder.) My mother informed all and sundry that that was no way for a lady to act. (Mother has never shirked from her duty to teach us manners.) Gerald retreated into his dinner plate (always quick to withdraw from uncomfortable situations). And I leapt into my role of peacemaker. We were busy being ourselves. The family was functioning normally.

This "being" business isn't always sunshine and roses. Being ourselves means that we are real people, warts and all. Being ourselves means that we make mistakes, get angry, feel pain, and hurt others. Being ourselves also means that we can laugh, love, and enjoy our lives. I have decided that the essence of survival when living with teenagers is to learn how to "be."

It also means allowing those teenagers to "be" as well. This wouldn't present any problems if they would "be" what I wanted; but as you and I know, there seems to be an unwritten law that a teenager will always be exactly the opposite of what you want. Maybe that's where all the conflict comes in when we have to deal with teenagers. Maybe that dichotomy of "being" is the real reason why I'm writing this book.

Nowhere is this dichotomy more evident than when it comes to career choices. I know I had some definite ideas for my children. Yet, at one point, Nathan had decided to be a short-order cook; Cherith was considering hairdressing; and Marnella was quite content with her part-time job at the local printing plant. Now there's nothing wrong with any of these career choices; they just weren't my career choices for the kids! I had something in mind like lawyers, doctors, and wildly successful entrepreneurs. I was willing to settle for model-of-the-year and a Nobel prize or two. Even a face on the cover of *Time* would have satisfied me.

I was having trouble allowing them to "be."

Well, all my efforts notwithstanding, by the time we reached the "kiss-off dinner," each of them had chosen his or her career path. Nathan is taking a recreation leadership course in college. He went in as a "mature" student because he didn't accrue enough high school credits to graduate. Cherith is finishing a "quickie" one-year office administration course—she wants to get it over with as fast as she can. Marnella is working on a home-study program for a C.G.A. (Certified General Accountant). So far, no lawyers on the horizon.

I'm working on "being" thankful that each is spreading his or her wings in his or her own way. It's not easy for an overachiever like me!

And Now for the Good News

I finally figured out how to "be." The answer lies in verses in the Bible called the Beatitudes. Look at them another way, and they could be called the "Be Attitudes." Taken separately, they give me the guidelines on how to be a parent of teenagers. Each attitude of being is a specific prescriptive on how to cope with—even survive—this phase of my life. Taken together, the Beatitudes form that self-help book that I knew had to exist somewhere. As Mother says, if you want to do something and if there's a book about it, you can do it!

2.
OPPKs

Blessed are the poor in spirit,
for theirs is the kingdom of heaven.
(Matthew 5:3)

Two

😐 _I've noticed that other people's kids are so much better than mine. In fact, it seems that they're darn near perfect! This is obvious from the yearly newsletters that I receive from my friends. These glowing reports speak of straight As, academic awards, outstanding achievements, musical genius, limitless talents, and cheerful dispositions. My own darlings pale in comparison to "other people's perfect kids" (OPPKs)._

It's especially bad at Christmas time when every second card contains the yearly accounting:

"Freddie is only seven, but academically, his teachers say he is at a grade five level."

"Our Christie surprised us all when she won three awards in the figure skating exhibitions."

"Billy prepared a five-course gourmet dinner for our anniversary last week."

"Kimberly will be attending Juilliard on a scholarship in the fall."

"Tom was voted most valuable player and received a letter for academic achievement as well."

"Tracey was editor of the school yearbook and the valedictorian for her class."

"Doug saved all his summer earnings and put them into a short-term investment account for his college expenses."

Sound familiar? It seems that everyone but me has kids who make writing a newsletter fun. I never write newsletters. What could I say?

"Cherith refused to be on any sports teams at school. She says she doesn't like getting all sweaty."

"Nathan spent his summer earnings on three new pairs of Reeboks."

"Marnella hasn't spoken to anyone for a week and spends all her time in her room."

"Cherith ran up a $100 long-distance bill last month."

"Nathan ditched the car last week while trying some fancy driving during a snowstorm."

"Our resident vegetarian, Marnella, now refuses to eat fish, except for lobster or crabmeat."

See what I mean? How can I possibly compete with the OPPKs? Of course, I could massage the facts and present them from another point-of-view. For example:

"Cherith has been too busy with her activities to give any time to the school teams."

"Nathan is often the fashion leader with his friends."

"Marnella amazes us with her self-discipline and determination."

"Cherith keeps in contact with an amazingly wide circle of friends."

"Nathan is experimenting with new driving techniques."

"Marnella continually introduces us to new culinary delights."

I guess it's all in the interpretation.

When my children entered high school, I thought that they would finally become the kind of kids that I could write about in a newsletter. I looked forward to making all my friends envious. Patiently, I waited for either or both of them to show outstanding academic achievement. No such luck.

As soon as she hit her first year, Cherith immediately changed her courses from the academic level (university entrance) to the general level (pre-community college). There wasn't anything I could do about it since our system allows the kids to make these changes themselves. In fact, the school doesn't even have to notify the parents. Cherith did achieve a few As, but I suspect that the ten-dollar reward had more to do with it than any desire to excel academically. She graduated comfortably in the middle of her class. Nathan hung in at the academic level and struggled bravely. Even so, he didn't manage enough credits to graduate.

Oh well, I consoled myself. There's more to school than straight As, things like sports, music, acting, writing, clubs, groups, and special interests. I remembered my own high school years: the drama club, the school band, the yearbook, cheerleading, and public speaking. I figured it was just a matter of time until something grabbed their attention. Nothing ever did. Meanwhile OPPKs were continuing to win awards, trophies, and scholarships.

I tried some gentle prodding. "Gee, Nathan, you could probably learn a lot of good guitar techniques in the school band. You might even be able to learn to play some other musical instruments." ("You've got to take music and write exams if you join the band. I don't need any more exams.")

"You know, Cherith, your modeling abilities would be enhanced if you were to join the drama club and learn some stage techniques." ("I'm not getting up there with a bunch of dorks and making a fool of myself.")

"Student Council?" ("Just a lot of hassle and work.")

"Cheerleading?" ("They look dumb with those baggy sweaters and short skirts.")

"Science Club?" ("I'm already taking chemistry.")

"Christian Club?" ("You've got to be kidding!")

I'm glad that my children are adopted. Otherwise, I would worry myself silly about genetic inheritance. For example, I can't say something like, "You're the only one in our family who has trouble with math." Having adopted them also means that I can't expect them to measure up to a bunch of standards that I have set based on my own experience and history. To some extent, they are freer than most kids to succeed or fail on their own merits.

I didn't realize this until Marnella moved in with us. As Gerald's natural child, she brought with her a lot of his traits and characteristics. But, she also brought a lot of expectations from Gerald. Several times, when she hadn't done what we expected, one or the other of us made a comment like, "It's hard to believe that she's yours (mine)," as if there is some divine blueprint that can never be changed. I think it's a lot harder for kids whose parents have that genetic pattern in mind when they begin to push their children in specific directions.

Certainly, it's a lot easier for me to excuse what I perceive as a failure to meet my expectations by reminding myself that I'm dealing with someone else's genetic history.

Maybe part of that pushing comes from all those newsletters we receive telling us about OPPKs. No one ever writes a newsletter that talks about children from a viewpoint other than what is acceptable. Yet when I think about it, I realize that my kids are just fine thank you, without all the awards, rewards, and trophies. (In fact, Nathan did receive a trophy as cub scout of the year when he was nine. Just thought I'd mention that.)

Why is it that I feel uncomfortable admitting that my children are less than perfect? Is it because I think that my own perfection as a parent is measured by their perfection as children? As long as my kids measure up to the standards that are set by others, then so do I. If they're okay, then I must be okay too.

Or could it be that I want to relive my life through my children? Do I vicariously enjoy a return to my teen years through their achievements and activities? Do I want to experience through them some of the things I missed when I was young? There's a whole lot more than just wanting something to put in the family newsletter that lies behind my desire for my children to excel.

If I let my expectations go and if I forget about OPPKs, I discover that I have a lot to make me proud. I have children who are their own persons, who haven't let me mold them into my perfect pattern. In fact, I have individuals here, not genetic clones that I have created.

They may not have the stuff that family newsletters seem to be made of, but taken in context, here are some kids who are perfect in their own right.

Cherith never joined anything at school. She didn't even go to the dances. But she has a wide circle of friends, and loves going out with them. She probably will never belong to the garden club, but she knows how to enjoy herself. Nathan refused to take music at school, but he has taught himself to play guitar and is now quite a musician—if you like modern noise. He won't be going to Juilliard, but he'll be playing for his own pleasure for the rest of his life. Marnella didn't want to go on to college— she said she was tired of school—but she has the self-discipline to study on her own and go for her own goals.

On the surface, my kids may not look too impressive when placed next to OPPKs. But underneath, I think I have the best of the bunch.

Now, I have to learn to let go and stop comparing them. I need to appreciate them for how they choose to be themselves, not for how they measure up against those OPPKs. I need to change my attitude from being uncomfortable with who my children are to being proud of the way each one of them is an individualist. I need to write a newsletter of my own.

And Now for the Good News 📖

When Jesus talks about the poor in spirit, he means a specific kind of poor. The Bible commentator Strong talks about it as being "destitute in wealth of learning and intellectual culture which the schools afford." Others see this attitude as one of "humbleness," without "position or honor in society." Either interpretation leads me to believe that my "Be Attitude" here is one of being free from comparisons with others and passing that freedom on to my children. I need to learn how to be poor in spirit: to be humble, accepting, and joyful with these teens in my care, not pushing them to provide me with vehicles for false pride.

3.
"Not My Kid!"

Blessed are those who mourn,
for they will be comforted.
(Matthew 5:4)

Three

☹ *I still remember the feelings in the pit of my stomach as I slipped the nail polish into my pocket: fear, excitement, guilt. I was convinced that every person in Woolworth's had witnessed my crime. I only made it through the door because Ella was right behind me, pushing me every time I hesitated. Outside, she exultantly opened her purse and pulled out several tubes of lipstick, some nail polish, and a scarf.*

"See, what did I tell you? It's easy," she said. Her look of triumph changed when I threw my stolen goods into the nearest trash bin. My life of crime had lasted no more than ten minutes.

I wish that I could tell you that I quit stealing because of my high moral standards, but the truth is I was afraid I would get caught. I wasn't concerned that if I got caught I might go to jail. That I could handle. But if I got caught, I would have to face my mother!

My mother is probably the most law-abiding person I know. More than that, she is totally honest. She expected no more and no less from me. I learned early on that it was better to tell the truth and face the consequences than to lie and be found out later (and she always found out!).

I tried to give the same message to my children: Honesty Pays. When my mother moved in with us, she took up where I left off. Once she sent Cherith to the store for some groceries and gave her a few pennies for some candy. When Cherith returned home, she had both the candy and the money. Mother asked her where she got the candy. Cherith claimed the storekeeper had given it to her and told her to keep the pennies. Mother didn't believe her (and neither did I since Cherith could tell a fib without batting an eyelash). Mother marched her right back down to the store and insisted that she confess her crime. Much to our embarrassment, it turned out that the storekeeper had indeed given her the candy (very out of character for this neighborhood curmudgeon). It seemed that our honesty lessons were paying off.

We had a similar experience with Nathan. He and a friend had decided to decorate a neighbor's car with eggs. They managed to dispose of a whole carton before they were found out. The neighbor was furious and threatened to call the police. We made Nathan go over to the man's house, apologize to him, and then wash his car. The neighbor agreed not to call the police. Bit by painful bit, the children were learning how to live within the law.

With some complacency I could smugly say, "not my kid," when others talked about their children's problems with the law.

Then, one evening when both Nathan and Cherith were spending the weekend at grandma's house in the city, I received a phone call that brought back memories of my brush with crime nearly forty years earlier. It was from the police. Cherith had been picked up for shoplifting and was in custody. Would I come down to the station?

It's hard to describe how I felt. First—angry. So angry. Then sad. But mostly just plain mad. It didn't help that we had a friend staying with us who chose this time to inform us how he (both childless and unmarried) would bring up children to respect the law. We were also in the middle of building our house, and I was covered in fiberglass dust from installing the insulation bats. The shower wasn't yet operational, so I had to clean up as best I could and find some clothes that portrayed a "responsible, caring parent."

By the time I got to the police station, I was in a royal state: dirty, itchy, and still mad. Cherith was waiting, pale and shaky (serves her right, I thought).

The policeman told me that her friend had been picked up several times before, but since this was Cherith's first offense (and last, I thought grimly), she hadn't been booked and would not have a record. Thank you, Lord, for small mercies.

In silence, we drove the thirty miles back to the farm. I didn't trust myself to speak until I could control my anger. Once home, Cherith headed for her room (just an unfinished shell with sheets for walls) and pulled the curtain over her doorway. She crawled into bed and turned her face to the wall.

I debated what to say.

"Why did you do it?" I knew why. Peer pressure. Excitement. Challenge. I'd been there once.

"How could you do this to me?" The embarrassment of having a criminal in the family would go far afield once our chatty guest hit the road.

"Who is this friend?" Just a kid from school. A kid who'd been over to my house for supper, for sleep overs. A kid whose parents drove her to hockey games and movies.

"What am I going to do with you?" I longed for the threat of the Home of the Good Shepherd. That had always been my mother's ultimate weapon. "I'm going to send you to the Home of the Good Shepherd." I knew that it was a place for wayward girls, although it was many years before I knew what wayward meant. However, my mother always assured me that I fit into the wayward category; and the nuns would be glad to have me. It wasn't a place that I wanted to go. I had seen the large brick building surrounded by a high fence, but I never saw any wayward girls on the grounds. I presumed that they were locked away in some dark underground cells.

The threat of the Home of the Good Shepherd always brought me in line. I decided I needed to give Cherith the same kind of incentive to walk the straight and narrow path. "Unless you can promise me that this will never happen again, I'm going to call the Social Services and tell them I can't control you. I'll ask them to place you in a foster home." I could hardly believe that I was making such a threat, but I knew that Cherith had some friends at school who were in foster homes; their lives were anything but pleasant. (However, as I looked around Cherith's half-finished bedroom, it occurred to me that a foster home might seem like an enticing alternative to her.)

Cherith didn't reply. "Think about it," I said sternly. "I want your promise."

It was a long weekend. Cherith stayed in her room, curled in a ball on her bed. Occasionally I would hear her crying. Everything in me longed to run in and comfort her, but I forced myself to ignore the impulse. This was something she had to deal with on her own. Only Cherith could make the decision to stay with us and abide by our rule, or to take her chances in a foster home.

On Sunday night she told me she was sorry, and it wouldn't happen again. I believed her. But a little part of me mourned for the lost innocence—not Cherith's, but mine. My naive belief that my children would never do anything that would lead them to a jail cell was gone. And my faith in how I was bringing up my children was shaken: I had lost control somewhere, and perhaps I would have to give up all control of my children and let strangers deal with them.

I do know that every parent mourns for that same lost innocence. Whether it is a brush with the law, a sexual encounter, an experiment with drugs, or a run-in with the school authorities, the parent can no longer proclaim, "Not my kid!"

Would I have sent Cherith into the strict hands of the Social Service authorities? Would my mother have sent me to the Home of the Good Shepherd? I don't know. I do mourn that these are decisions that parents have to make—that I have to make. I mourn for the family that I had imagined I would have— one like that of Ward and June Cleaver. Somehow, I can't see June bailing the Beaver out of jail!

And Now for the Good News 📖

It's hard to admit that my child is no better, and no worse, than any other. The only edge I can give him or her is my abiding love, tempered with discipline. It is the same kind of love that my father in heaven gives to me.

My "Be Attitude" tells me that it is all right to mourn for these things because the God of all Comfort brings me through the tough times into a life of loving reality.

4.
Why Me?

Blessed are the meek,
for they will inherit the earth.
(Matthew 5:5)

Four

😐 *I had never planned to get into the mother-hood business. For one thing, I didn't have any previous business experience. Being an only child, I had enjoyed a sibling-free life; and I carefully avoided any neighborhood baby-sitting jobs.*

In my adult years, I didn't coo over new babies. I didn't ask to hold them, and I certainly didn't covet the privilege of feeding and/or changing the little dears. In short, I had neither the experience nor inclination in this field of endeavor.

Pregnancy didn't happen in the first years of my marriage. Frankly, I was somewhat relieved that nature withheld this favor from me. Shortly after our sixth anniversary, Mervyn and I decided that we really didn't want children; so he underwent "the operation." I think we both breathed a little easier.

Then, three years later, Mervyn suggested that we adopt a child. He had been praying with a friend, and they both felt this was the direction that God wanted us to take. Who was I to argue with God? So I agreed. This was in March. On June 22, Nathan arrived.

He was small, smelly, and squalling. I didn't even know how to hold him. I made a 1,500-mile long-distance call to my mother and followed her step-by-step instructions for bathing, feeding, and changing him.

Why me?

Nathan and I survived our first year together. I put on thirty stress pounds, and he eventually learned to sleep for more than two hours at a time. Shortly after Nathan's first birthday, we decided to adopt another child. I thought a second boy would be easier, having one "under my belt" so to speak. Mother suggested a girl as a change of scene. On June 12, nearly a year to the day from Nathan, Cherith came into our lives.

I still remember sitting in a Holiday Inn restaurant where we had stopped after "picking up" our child. We eagerly unwrapped our new baby. As layer after layer of clothing came off (she was wearing her entire government-issued layette), we realized that our roly-poly bundle was the longest, skinniest baby we had ever seen!

Two children, exactly a year apart, kept me busy for the next three years. Then, when Nathan was five and Cherith four, Mervyn and I were divorced.

I was now on my own, the sole bread-winner, chief cook and bottle-washer, single parent, and divorced woman.

Why me?

We survived. Six years later I remarried. Now I had an added title: stepmother. Although Gerald's daughter lived with her mother, she still spent many weekends with us. It was a whole new kind of parenting as we struggled make her feel a part of our blended family.

I guess we succeeded. When she was eighteen, Marnella moved in with us. I was now the frazzled mother of three teenagers.

Why me?

Looking back, I realize that I did it all wrong. I was so eager to make the new arrangement work that I forgot that the word "no" existed.

Marnella wanted to bring her pets: three cats, four fat fish, and three turtles (each the size of a dinner plate). Sure. Why not? The more the merrier. I didn't say a word. Even when one of the turtles escaped, only to turn up in the back of my closet a day or two later, I said nothing. (Can you imagine what it is like to be rooting among your shoes in search of a mate to the one on your left foot, and coming eye to eye with a cold reptilian gaze that looks suspiciously like that of a large snake?)

Marnella had specific ideas about what her room should be like. We moved Nathan out of the large front bedroom and completely redecorated it to her requirements, right down to the new hardwood floor. When her things didn't fit, she spilled over onto the landing and into the storage room next door. I bit my tongue as I stumbled over the cats' litter box. I said nothing at the clothing hung over the banister to dry. I was being Mrs. Wonderful Stepmother.

Marnella was a vegetarian. No problem. I cooked two meals every evening—an exercise that grew increasingly difficult as time plainly revealed that Marnella wasn't a vegetarian. She didn't like vegetables. Finally, I managed to figure out what she did like: plain pizza, plain spaghetti, (and I mean plain—no onions, no green peppers, no mushrooms, just cheese and tomato sauce), canned beans (vegetarian style, of course), Kraft dinner, canned macaroni and noodles, ice cream, and cereals. I fussed and fumed and worried that she wasn't getting the nutrients she needed to remain healthy. I tried to sneak in tofu—she found it. I tried to add eggs—she knew. I tried tuna—no way! And still I made two meals each evening.

Marnella was environmentally concerned. She didn't use the clothes dryer—a waste of energy. I ignored the racks of wet clothing that festooned the upper hallway. She didn't use bleaches, softeners, or detergents. My boxes of baking soda and bottles of vinegar disappeared without warning, no doubt to be used as environmentally safe substitutes.

She was an only child who had lived quite independently in her own apartment in her mother's townhouse. She had had her own bathroom, her own space, and her own life. I held back my anger when she flitted into the bathroom just as everyone else was also getting ready for school. I gritted my teeth when loud rock music echoed from her 1000-megawatt stereo system. I bit back comments when she insisted on watching her favorite television programs, which meant that the one and only television antenna was tuned in the opposite direction for the program I was watching.

Don't for a moment think that my little darlings didn't take advantage of Mom's sudden fit of Mrs. Wonderful Stepmother. Both insisted on having their bedrooms redone too. Cherith got an expensive pink carpet that really wasn't necessary; Nathan got his entire body-building gym set in his room.

Both discovered the fun of eating whatever you wanted from the refrigerator without bothering to check with Mom, just in case it was something she had planned later. And they both loved trying to one-up Marnella when it came to sheer noise volume from their own megawatt loudspeaker stereo systems.

All three figured that the resident maid and butler should do the housework. Dishes piled up, the bathrooms were a disgrace, and the litter box was more than just a grace note in the air when you came into the house.

In a fit of desperation, Gerald and I set up a duty roster and posted it on the refrigerator. The three of them just ignored it.

Finally, I broke. I yelled. I screamed. I threatened. Gerald backed me up with a silent, simmering anger that was a lot more effective than all my noise. They got the message. Reluctantly, they took on some of the responsibilities for keeping the house livable. But never, ever, did they do one iota more than required by the duty roster.

And on all other fronts, we were the losers. The food still disappeared from the refrigerator with alarming speed: several quarts of milk a day, an entire bunch of bananas within hours, a box of cookies overnight. Noise continued to reverberate throughout the house: three tape decks, one compact disc player, three televisions, two record players, umpteen radios, and Nathan's guitar and accompanying amplifier, complete with wahwah pedal. Hot water was at a premium. Even with a strict shower and laundry schedule, at any given moment, the hot water would simply give out just as either my body or Gerald's stood naked and covered with soap in a steaming shower stall.

And cars! I had, of course, in my Mrs. Wonderful Stepmother guise, allowed Marnella complete access to my car. I didn't want her to feel trapped on the farm after the freedom of her big-city life. When Nathan got his driver's license, the battles began. One car, two teenagers, and an insurance bill that could easily have paid off our mortgage clouded our days. The only silver lining to this particular cloud was Cherith's outright refusal to learn to drive a standard-shift car. I shudder to think of what would have happened if she had jumped into the car fray.

Why me?

I should have remembered to say "no." Being Mrs. Wonderful Stepmother (or just plain Wonderful Mom) is a big mistake. I was so sure that I had to meekly endure all that landed on my plate, I forgot that it is also my job to set guidelines, establish ground rules, and make sure that everyone knows what the bottom line is for living in my house.

I've always known that I am an assertive lady. It's a reason that Gerald jokingly refers to me as Miss Bossy-Boots. Yet for three years, I never said a word. I was afraid of upsetting Marnella. I was afraid of what others might say about me if she were to run back to Mother. That fear made me weak, *not* meek.

The meekness that Jesus asks of me is that of a gentle person, not occupied by self at all. It should stem from a complete trust in God's goodness and control over any situation. I should be able to accept all His dealings with me as good, without disputing or worrying over them. This means that I should be able to meekly hand the whole mess over to Jesus.

I did eventually reach this state. When I began to suffer from severe arthritis in my knees and back, I realized that I was burying my anger and resentment in my body. It was time to do something. I tried yelling at Gerald. He simply retreated. I tried yelling at my children. They began to talk about leaving home. Since my job took me out of town, I tried working myself silly, but my body just couldn't keep up the pace. Finally, in desperation, I gave Marnella, my anger, and the complete chaos of my household to Jesus. "It's all yours," I told Him. "I give up."

I became meek.

Within months Marnella found a good job, a good apartment, and a good life for herself in the city. She, the turtles, one cat, and half of her belongings and a moving van left on a bright September morning. We parted friends.

Today, I sit in my clean house surrounded by the sounds of the birds in the tree outside my window. The refrigerator is full, the water is hot, and the car is idle in the driveway. The empty nest is never sweeter than it is as I look back on the last three years.

And Now for the Good News 📖

I still have trouble with the meek "Be Attitude." I've never been good at "letting go and letting God," but I know that's the secret to this particular attitude. Meekness doesn't mean letting someone (a teenager, for instance) walk all over you. Meekness means giving the anger and the resentment to Jesus. How much easier it would be if I could learn to adopt the attitude of meekness before I reach the end of my rope. Meekness means that I can rely on God's strength to deal with whatever conditions I face.

5.

Necessary Things

*Blessed are those who
hunger and thirst for righteousness,
for they will be filled.*
(Matthew 5:6)

Five

☹ *One thing I know about teenagers is that they hunger and thirst for all the things of this world. At any moment they will have a list of "things" that are necessary to make their lives complete. Usually this list evolves from a combination of what everyone else has, what the latest items are, and what they believe they deserve.*

Nathan has always felt that we fall far short of the acceptable motorized limits in our neighborhood. In the winter, we are the only family for miles around without a snowmobile. To Nathan's disgust, we opt for cross-country skis instead of combustion-engine mayhem in the woods. In the summer, our canoe is an anomaly among all the motorboats on our lake. Nathan just can't understand it.

Cherith, on the other hand, bemoans our lack of color televisions complete with umpteen stations from a satellite dish in the backyard. Where are VCRs, CD players and camcorders? She also tells us that we are the only family on our block (side-road) that doesn't have a gas barbecue, matching patio chairs, and an in-ground swimming pool.

Marnella suffers greatly from our lack of bathroom space. She can't understand why we simply don't install another bathroom or two, complete with a Jacuzzi and whirlpool tub.

All three agree that we should have a car available for their use: something sporty, something flashy, something with power steering, power stereo, and a full tank of gas. (The old standard-shift Chevy that sits in our driveway just isn't up to their standards—and it always needs to have the gas tank filled.)

Life sure is tough for the have-nots!

It doesn't stop at cars and swimming pools and Jacuzzi bathrooms. At no point do we measure up to the acceptable standards of what is necessary to their lives and sense of well-being.

Clothes are only acceptable when they bear a particular label. Anything else is below standard. I did once toy with the idea of starting a small label production company. I would sell other long-suffering parents a life-time's supply of designer labels, complete with a peel and stick washable backing that could be used and reused as clothes were recycled. The idea had definite possibilities.

No matter what I buy, unless it meets the label criteria, it is not a wearable item. The closets in this house are full of clothes that have never seen the light of day, simply because they were the wrong brand. Style, color, price, even popularity, are irrelevant. No label: no wear.

Food is another item of controversy. It was bad enough when the battles were waged over Frosty Chocolate Nutsy Loops versus corn flakes, but now we have moved to a whole new level of food discrimination. Gourmet (read expensive and almost impossible to obtain) is in. Breakfast is not a corn flakes affair: it must be imported granola with macadamia nuts. An apple a day no longer does the trick; they want kiwi fruit, passion fruit, or papaya. Forget cheese slices. We're looking at imported Gorgonzola, Edam, or Cheshire cheese. Bread isn't white; it's seven-grain brown, hand-mixed, stone-baked, individually wrapped, and free from preservatives, coloring, and calories.

They don't want plain ice cream. They want the super-deluxe gourmet, pure chocolate made with real cream. They don't want tuna (dolphin-safe or otherwise), but crab meat, shrimp paste, or lobster pieces for their lunch boxes.

Forget margarine: it's creamery butter (dairy-fresh and salt-free) on that seven-grain bread. Don't try for ketchup: it's the Mexican salsa, or Italian pesto, or British sauce that does the trick on the hamburgers. Speaking of which, don't bother with those handy patties from the freezer. They want lean-ground beef, hand-formed and fat-free on their bakery-bought, poppy seed buns.

McDonald's is great when they're little, but teenagers only go to McDonald's when they're the ones who are paying. If Mom and Dad are treating, then it's on to one of the new up-scale "yuppie" restaurants where they can experiment with shrimp cocktails, surf and turf platters, or French-silk pie.

Generic clothes, generic sodas, and generic vacations are out!

No matter how hard I try to keep up to their standards, it's never enough. At one point, I bought a small above-ground swimming pool, one of those Sears Roebuck and Company catalog items that require no special plumbing and no installation.

This thrilled the kids—for all of twelve minutes. Then, it was too small, too shallow, too crowded, too flimsy, too inadequate for their needs.

Several years later Gerald and I bought a larger above-ground pool, one that required special plumbing and experts to install. It was great—for about one summer. Then, it didn't have a pool heater, or a pool cleaner (other than the resident maid and butler), or a diving board, or a deck. It just wasn't measuring up.

For one mad moment we actually thought about an in-ground installation. Fortunately, we took the time to assess what the pool meant to us—the pool-payers, so to speak—and we discovered that we never had time to swim in it. When we did, it was full of kids. We were the ones who scrubbed and cleaned it, kept the chemicals in balance, vacuumed it, topped it up, opened it in spring, and closed it in winter. We were *not* the ones who wanted a pool in the first place. When we sold the farm, we left the old above-ground pool behind.

It's the same with almost every other "necessary thing" in their lives. I remember the first color television we had: it was a secondhand set with a dodgy vertical hold. But we were thrilled to have it. Then, along came the teen years. How come we only had a seventeen-inch screen when everyone else had a twenty-four-inch one? How come we only had one television set? How come we didn't have a satellite dish in the back yard? How come we didn't have a VCR?

So, we bought another television. Now we had one in the family room and one in the kitchen. How come we didn't have a television in each bedroom like everyone else? We installed a television tower and antenna that allowed us to pull in a few more stations. Why couldn't we run cable lines to every room? We finally got ourselves a VCR. How come we didn't have a camcorder to record our own movies to show on the VCR?

How did this happen? Where did I go wrong? Where did my children get the idea that *things* are necessary for enjoying life? Certainly, I wanted them to have a better life than I had. That is a common desire among all parents. Surely that in itself does not constitute a life based on having *things*?

Futurists tell us that this will be the first generation that doesn't have a higher standard of living than their parents. I don't believe it. They already have a higher standard of living than I ever dreamed of having. They have it in my house!

Perhaps that is why so many children are returning to the nest. We've made it just too comfortable for them. Marnella lasted just six months on her own. Then, she packed it all up and returned to her mother's house in Montreal. There were many reasons for the move, but her one comment was very telling. "I was living in poverty on my own. Rent, hydro, telephone, food, and cable just cost too much. There wasn't any left over for me." Now it's all left over for her. Her standard of living has definitely gone up.

Many of my friends are complaining about this return-to-the-nest phenomenon. Some of them have thirty-five-year-old fledglings living with them! I keep telling them that the nest is just too darn comfortable. Why would anyone want to leave a life with live-in maid, cook and butler service, cable television, use of a car, gourmet meals, laundry facilities, and unlimited freedom? Come to think of it, maybe I could move back in with my mother.

I've tried to give my children some idea of what it is like in the real world. They've always had to pay me room and board whenever they have worked during the summer. The money usually returned to them in the form of school clothes, tuition, or books. Their friends were horrified that they had to *pay* their own parents to live in their own home. I know it has made a difference in how they view the cost of living on the outside.

(I didn't do that for Marnella. It was a mistake. She went unprepared for the cost of freedom. I didn't do her any favors by waiving my rule of "paying your own way.")

Somewhere, somehow, I hope that I have given my children the idea that *things* do not matter. Having said that, I have to sheepishly admit that the moment they had some money of their own, they each rushed out to buy *things*.

And Now for the Good News

This is one of the "Be Attitudes" I find easiest to live. I really do not measure my life by the things in it. I have always said that I could walk away from it all today if it were necessary. To hunger and thirst for righteousness is simply to lay up treasure in heaven, not here on earth. By continually doing so, I present to my children a model of "being" that is so radically different from what they see in the world around them, they can't help but notice.

6.
McJob Or McWelfare

Blessed are the merciful,
for they will receive mercy.
(Matthew 5:7)

Six

☺ *I got my first job when I was thirteen. I was hired to be a companion for a nine-year-old over the summer. Her mother worked and needed someone during the days. I was that someone.*

I can't even remember the little girl's name. I do remember hating the job, probably hating the little girl, and wishing that I hadn't jumped at the chance to make a few dollars. But I stuck it out. Quitting wasn't allowed in our house.

I worked every summer after that, starting as a playground supervisor and ending up as a senior counselor in a residential camp. It never occurred to me *not* to work in the summer.

When I left school, I got my first full-time job. I have worked more or less continually since then: over thirty years with only a break here and there. My mother has also worked all her life. So has my husband. So do most of my friends. We are all of generations that ascribe to the work ethic. I presumed that it would be the same with my children.

Not so. They don't like work. More than that, they don't want to work because it cuts into their social life and cramps their style. It's not just my children. It's the whole generation. I keep reading about these teenagers who are holding down part-time jobs while going to school, but I haven't met any yet. All the ones I know wouldn't be caught dead working on valuable weekend time.

During the summer, the issue of a job becomes a major source of conflict in our house. The first year they were sixteen, I told Nathan and Cherith they needed to find jobs. No one moved. I reminded them to get some resumes into the mail. Nothing happened. I told them to sign up at the Youth Employment Office. No one did.

Then, I got mad and they got jobs. Cherith got a job in the local tourism booth, dispensing aid and advice to the hordes of people who invade our tourism area each summer. Nathan went to work as a maintenance person at his old church camp.

The next summer, Cherith went to stay with her grandmother in the city on the pretext of having a better chance of getting a job. After two weeks of inactivity, I personally drove her down to the Youth Employment Bureau, filled out her application, found a job on the board for her, called for an appointment and drove her there. She got the job.

Nathan didn't have much luck, but finally agreed to take on odd jobs from the employment office board. There he found Mr. Doolittle, a local cottager, who has kept Nathan in pocket money through odd jobs for the last three years. He also found a full-time job as an attendant at the local gas station. It was another summer of employed teenagers. I secretly congratulated myself.

The next summer, Cherith returned to her grandmother's again. This time, she had no intention of getting a job and managed very nicely not to do so. I was up to my ears in building a new house and didn't have my usual time and energy to do the hunting for her. Cherith spent a lovely, idle summer, and came home with a very nice tan.

Nathan, however, was still at home. I found the time to drive him to the employment center. He took a job as a counselor at the local day camp, a job of minimum wage earnings that he supplemented with his growing cottage clientele (thanks to Mr. Doolittle).

Meanwhile, Marnella had moved in. She indicated that she thought she needed a little vacation to recover from the stress and strain of moving, but after three weeks, when she told us she didn't want to return to college, we persuaded her to look for a local job. She found a part-time job (only three days a week) that suited her just fine. It provided her with enough money for life's little necessities, but it didn't take up too much of her personal time, which she needed for her own private pursuits. When the job went down to two days a week, she continued on. It was too much bother to change jobs and didn't look good on a resume to have a lot of short-lived jobs, she explained.

Meanwhile, Cherith graduated from college. She had a certificate in office administration, and I waited for her to start work. She didn't.

I wrote a resume for Cherith and made fifty copies. I got the names and addresses of every possible company that might want office help. Then I gave her the money for a roll of stamps, gave her a package of large envelopes, and sent her on her way.

Nothing happened. There are no jobs, she informed me. None in the paper, none in the stores, and none on the job board in the employment center. I decided to take her for lunch, and then visit the center and see for myself. On the way, we saw a friend of hers who had also been looking for a job. "Come for lunch," I invited.

"I can't," she said. "I'm just on my way to work."

"Oh, did you get a job?" I asked.

"Yes. Tim Horton's Doughnut shop hired me. It's just minimum wage, but the tips are great. I'm working three to eleven which pretty much ruins my evenings, but it's a job. You should try there,

Cherith," she continued. "They're still hiring, and with your experience, you'll probably get on."

Cherith gave her a look that would have frozen a lesser person to stone.

In the restaurant, I suggested that after lunch I could drive Cherith to the donut shop; there she could fill out an application.

"I don't want to work there. It's just a McJob. And it's at night. I don't want to have to work in the evenings. And there'll be weekend work too."

I dropped the subject, and at that moment dropped all pretense of believing that Cherith really wanted a job. "Do what you want," I said.

What she wanted, it turned out, was to go on welfare until she could find the kind of job she wanted. Again, I bit my tongue. "That's your decision," I said.

A week later she called to tell me that she had had her first interview with the welfare office and that a check was on its way. I said nothing. She started to talk about getting an apartment. I said nothing. She reminded me that I had promised her a new bedroom set as a graduation present. I said nothing. She mentioned the need to have first and last month's rent available. I asked her where she planned to get it. Well, I had said I would help her when she was ready to set up her own apartment.

I said something. I started by saying how I felt about welfare and ended by telling her that I had done many McJobs in my life simply to provide food for her little rosebud mouth. I said it all.

I hung up wondering if my daughter would ever talk to me again. I had tried so hard to let her work out her own future, but when it got right down to the core of how I felt, I couldn't refrain from being critical. Being honest about how I felt about Cherith's choices was probably one of the best things I could have done.

That afternoon she called back to say that she had applied at Tim Horton's. Three weeks later, she was hired. She works five days a week on the three to eleven shift. Two of those days are weekends. She doesn't like the hours, the minimum wages, or the uniform. It's a McJob.

I'm sure that part of the reason so many teenagers want to avoid the job market is simply because there isn't much of a market out there. I can remember having my pick of jobs. Today, however, if a kid finds a McJob, he or she is fortunate. A friend's daughter, who is now twenty-six, has never worked. She doesn't like going for interviews, she says. I don't blame her. These kids have more rejections before they're twenty than I've had in a lifetime. Her husband can't find a job either. Together, they live in subsidized housing, eking out their welfare checks with visits to the food bank and the thrift store. This isn't the standard of living they were used to at home.

Another friend struggled and scraped to put her daughter through college and was as proud as punch when she graduated with a degree in Russian language and economics. Today, her daughter is living at home and works as a check-out clerk at the local supermarket. The choice is limited: McJob or McWelfare.

It might not have seemed as if I was showing mercy to my children when I pushed them to work at whatever job was available to them. But I was. I know that it is more merciful to teach them that any work is better than no work. One day the welfare cushion will no longer be available, and for those who have not learned to grab at the first available McJob, it will be a day of tough reckoning.

And Now for the Good News

The "Be Attitude" of mercy is not a soft attitude. It is more merciful in the long-run to be tough-minded and honest than it is to go along with the way our world copes with life's problems. God shows the same kind of mercy to me. His tough-love strengthens me for the tough times that I have ahead. Without it, I would falter and fail.

7.
My Way

Blessed are the pure in heart,
for they will see God.
(Matthew 5:8)

__Seven__

☺ *"As long as you're in my house, under my roof, eating my food, you'll do things my way." Sound familiar? Every parent has used that line at one time or another, usually when the teenager has just done the exact opposite of your way. If every parent uses this line, every teenager hates to hear it. "Just you wait," he or she mutters. "One day I won't be in your house, and I'll do just what I want to."*

Clothes, curfews, chores, and friends can all drive me to this age-old last line of parental self-defense. Yet, the teenager still finds a way to circumvent "my way" and leaves me feeling angry and resentful.

Take the issue of clothes. It's bad enough that my teenagers all insist on brand names and the latest fashion fads, but they also use clothes as a weapon against "my way." By the time she was fourteen,

Cherith really didn't want to go to church anymore. However, she knew better than to open up that can of worms with old "my way" Mom, so she settled for a subtle sabotage. She began to dress for church as if she were heading for the nearest disco bar: short skirts that barely covered her bottom, tight tops (preferably in black lace), three-inch heels and full runway makeup. (I'd like to make it clear that most of these ensembles came from "trades" with friends—another subtle sabotage of "my way").

Every Sunday morning I was torn. Do I confront her with the inappropriateness of her clothes and demand she put on something else? This would give her an excuse to say that the church didn't allow her to be herself, and we were all a bunch of hypocrites anyway. Or, do I ignore her choice of clothes and watch the members of the ladies' aid (not to mention their husbands) lose their eyebrows in their hairlines?

The problem was her clothing proclaimed her to be something that I knew she wasn't. But did everyone else know the real Cherith too? How did her clothing choice reflect on me as her parent? I knew that she chose those clothes just to shock others and to annoy me. It worked!

Cherith did the same thing with her friends. She knew just how to tie me up neatly in "my way." If I said I didn't like her friends, I was being un-Christian. I knew that if I put my foot down, just forbidding a friendship pretty well guaranteed that Cherith would cling to it like grim death. So, I learned to bite my tongue. I bit my tongue when Nikky shared her version of the facts of life with Cherith. I bit my tongue when Tammi persuaded Cherith to swap her dress slacks for a pair of Tammi's skin-tight jeans. I bit my tongue when Cheryl arrived for the sleep over complete with cigarettes. I bit my tongue when Dave borrowed money from Cherith and never paid it back. I bit my tongue when Sean turned out to be a lot older than I had been led to believe. My tongue got mighty sore!

Nathan also learned how to use some subtle sabotage when Mom began singing the "my way" blues. When he got old enough to bring girls home, I announced that he could only entertain a girl in his room if he left the door wide open. (I'm not sure that I really considered the unlikeliness of any hanky-panky behind closed doors in a household with one nosy dog, two pushy sisters, three in-and-out felines, and a set of watchful parents.) I figured an open door would put a damper on any teenage ardor.

Nathan let me know how he felt about the rules. The door stayed open all right, but we were all treated to a concert of "music' on his electric guitar, complete with bass-pounding amplifiers and a wah-wah pedal (which does exactly what it sounds like).

Within minutes, someone would shout, "If you're going to make that racket, shut the door!" And the winner is . . .

When Marnella moved in with us, I started out by gently letting her know about "my way." Well, maybe not in so many words, but the essence was there.

My censorship stopped at the door of Marnella's bedroom. As a nineteen-year-old, she could read books, watch television, and listen to music that I didn't like. One day our friends arrived and were greeted with a rock ballad pulsing down the stairs from her upstairs room. I can't even write the lyrics, much less repeat them to someone of my generation. They definitely weren't "my way."

I suppose I tried to institute the rules for the same reason as every parent does: I wanted my children to be pure—pure in mind, body, and spirit. I wanted them to have the purity that comes from being free from the corruptions of our age, free from modern fashions, modern music, and modern manners. I also wanted the rest of the world to know that they were pure—this would reflect back on me and my wonderful parenting abilities.

However, my children have to live in this world. No amount of preaching on my part can protect them. I can loudly announce the "under my roof" statement, and it doesn't make one bit of a difference. They're going to do it "their way," and that's all there is to it.

I knew that I was clutching at straws when I glowingly described Cherith's boyfriend as "never married, not a father, and not even on parole." It's as close to "my way" as we're likely to get.

And Now for the Good News

I guess it all boils down to what's inside. I fuss and fume about those outward appearances, but I know that all the time my children have spent in a Christian atmosphere must make a difference to what's on the inside. My "Be Attitude" is to maintain the purity of my own heart in the face of all that I see daily.

8.

Would You Like a Cup of Tea?

*Blessed are
the peacemakers, for they will be
called children of God.*
(Matthew 5:9)

Eight

🙁 *What is it about teenagers that brings out the beast in perfectly reasonable, sensible adults? One word, one facial expression, one curl of the lip, even a simple sigh can strip away the veneer of civilization and expose a deep-seated aggression that the parent never suspected lurked in his or her heart.*

My mother, like me, has a fairly volatile temper, but she tends to express it with a loud voice and the occasional thrown tea cup. I would never call her a violent person. Yet, once when I told one of her friends to "go to H- E- double hockey sticks," my mother grabbed the nearest thing she could find to spank me with. (I was nearly twelve at the time, so her hand would have been somewhat ineffective.) Unfortunately, the nearest item was the dog leash. Two good swipes across the back of my legs left welts that lasted for days. Poor Mom was appalled at the welts and even more so when I made sure that everyone around saw my "battered" body. No doubt, those who didn't know her thought she was some kind of out-of-control virago who regularly beat her poor, defenseless daughter.

Like all teenage daughters and their mothers, my mother and I had our battles. However, we had a formula for peacemaking. When the dust had cleared, one of us would make a pot of tea. The invitation, "Would you like a cup of tea?" was our truce signal. It was an unwritten rule that you never turned down the offer. Over tea, we sorted out our difficulties and got back on track. Sometimes we drank a lot of tea!

No one escapes from these teen-triggered explosions of rage. When I was in my early twenties, I lived for a short time with a minister and his family. I presumed that I was going to a heaven-like place with no tempers, no anger, and no battles. I was wrong.

The Armstrongs had four children, and the eldest, Mary, was just thirteen—a dangerous age when life becomes a constant battle of wills between teenager and parent. Most of the disagreements were limited to minor skirmishes, but occasionally an out-and-out war would break out.

Mornings were always a little tense. June worked full time, and Ron drove her to the bus on his way to the church office. All four children had to be up, dressed, fed, and on their way to school before Ron and June left the house.

Despite the rush, breakfast was a sit-down family affair. One morning, everything was running behind schedule. June was trying to get the youngest to eat his toast, the next one to find her lunch box, and number three to change into a clean blouse. Mary arrived late, plunked herself down, filled up her cereal bowl, and said to no one in particular, "Pass the milk."

No one responded. Then Mary's voice went up a notch: "I said, 'Pass the milk'." She hesitated and loudly added, "Please."

"Just a minute," June said as she wiped up some spilled jam.

"I need the milk *now*." Mary's voice emphasized the last word, and then she added the final touch. "That is, if you can drag yourself away from your own food long enough to pass it to me." At this point, June had yet to have a mouthful of her own breakfast.

Without hesitation, June reached over, picked up the milk pitcher, and poured the contents on Mary's head! "Is that enough milk for you?" she asked sweetly. See what I mean about uncivilized responses?

Ron never seemed to get into these frays. I put it down to the fact that he was (a) a minister, and (b) a morning person. He rose early, and the rest of us were usually awakened by a loud tenor rendition of his hymn for the day. He was invariably cheerful, never ruffled, and on top of things from 5:00 a.m. on. I don't think I ever saw him really angry. I decided that even temper was part of a minister's emotional makeup.

For this reason, perhaps only ministers could withstand the temptation to revert to their animal natures when dealing with teens. This idea was unequivocally wiped out one Saturday morning when I heard an altercation downstairs in the hallway. It was Ron's voice I heard, not raised in song, but raised in angry protest! Mary was supposed to do the laundry, but she wanted to go out first. Ron didn't agree. Mary finally got in the last word, "and you can't make me," she yelled. Ron grabbed the broom and literally shooed her down to the laundry room with a few well-aimed swats. "I'll report you to the Children's Aid," Mary screamed as she began bundling clothes into the washer. "Fine," said Ron. "Just as soon as you finish the laundry, I'll drive you down there myself." So much for my idea that Christians were immune from such behavior!

Despite all the evidence to the contrary, I knew that when I became a parent, I would never treat my children that way. I was convinced that I could remain reasonable and in control of the situation, whatever the provocation might be. That was before I had teens of my own.

Cherith was mouthy. Not overtly, but the mumbling-under-the-breath kind of mouthy that drives a parent wild. Accompanied by her famous pout and hair toss, one mumbled remark would trigger insane desires to pour milk over her head or chase her around the room with a broom.

But I prided myself on my restraint and limited myself to a sharp, "What did you say?" Then I derived some satisfaction when she backed down with a sullen, "Nothing."

One day Cherith wanted to go out with her friend up the road. "Not until you do the dishes," I said. "It's your turn," Gerald reminded her. She mouthed something under her breath.

"What did you say?" Gerald demanded. She didn't answer.

"Well," I pushed.

Cherith repeated her remark, loud enough for both Gerald and me to hear. I don't even remember what she said, but I do know that Gerald and I lunged at her simultaneously. She nimbly side-stepped us and in a second, was out the kitchen door. We were right on her heels. Down the driveway we went: first Cherith, then Gerald, then me. I wasn't chasing Gerald to stop him. I wanted to get that young lady myself. Round and round the lawn we ran. What a spectacle we made as her friend arrived. No doubt it's a scenario that Karen still describes whenever the subject of child abuse comes up.

By the time Cherith had enough sense to stop and face the music, Gerald and I were too out of breath to do anything but ground her for the day. I often wonder what would have happened if Gerald had caught her first—or if I had!

My only comfort is to remind myself that Jesus reacted with anger when driven to right a wrong. When he threw the money changers out of the temple, he didn't stop to reason with them first! I wonder if Jesus regretted his angry actions, just as I often do.

I don't think that my children have been emotionally scarred by these angry outbursts. Although Marnella still talks about the time Gerald tossed her in her wading pool to cool off her smart aleck mouth, she doesn't bear a grudge and has even admitted that she probably deserved a good soaking. Cherith still remembers our marathon around the lawn and can even laugh about it now. And I still remind Mom that she beat me, but only when I'm also reminding her what a model child I was.

And Now for the Good News

Maybe I've hit upon the "Be Attitude" here. It is to be a peacemaker—to literally forgive and forget; to put those angry moments behind us. So many of us hang on to our anger, regurgitating it in bitter memories that dim the joy of our present relationships. To be a peacemaker is simply to offer (or accept) that cup of tea and start anew.

9.

What Part of "No" Don't You Understand?

*Blessed are those who
are persecuted for righteousness' sake,
for theirs is the kingdom of heaven.*
(Matthew 5:10)

<u>Nine</u>

☹ *I have a reputation among my children's friends of being a "party pooper." I came by it honorably: my mother had the same reputation with my friends! You see, I don't always go along with the popular point-of-view when it comes to kids and what they want. Neither did my mom.*

When I was fifteen, the Saturday night movie in town was a given. Everyone went with or without dates. It ended at 11:00, the last bus home left at 11:30, and I was home by 12:00.

Then, the movie house brought in "Midnight Movies." After the evening crowd left, those who wanted to could stay on and another movie was shown at midnight. Staying for the midnight movie became the "in" thing. But I couldn't do that. I always had to leave in order to catch the last bus home. One Saturday night my girlfriends and I met some friends who had a car. They assured me that they would drive me home.

I called my mother and asked her if I could stay. Without missing a beat, she said "no." I argued; I pleaded; I begged. She was adamant. My curfew was midnight, and that was that. In a moment of rebellion, I informed her that I was staying; and since we lived six miles out of town and she didn't have a car, there wasn't a darn thing she could do about it. I hung up the phone feeling very adult and independent. My friends and I settled back to wait for the midnight movie to start.

Ten minutes into the movie, the lights went on, the movie projection stopped, and the movie manager got up on the stage to make an announcement. He called out my name. Completely mystified, I stood up and found myself the object of every pair of eyes in the theatre as a policeman beckoned me and then marched me up the aisle. My mother had sent the police to get me! I was underage, so legally wasn't supposed to be out after midnight, a law that was never enforced in our town. But Mom had a friend whose husband was a policeman, and he expedited the unusual "arrest." I was driven home and deposited on the doorstep where my angry mother was waiting.

My mother's reputation as party pooper was now firmly established, and I learned one valuable lesson from the experience: "no" means no. It's a lesson I've tried hard to teach my own children.

Usually, the lesson comes from a situation where "everyone else is doing it." Just once, I wish I could get a list of who "everyone else" is. To listen to my teens, the belief is that it encompasses every person in a hundred mile radius. I suspect it actually means one lone adult who has been talked (conned) into saying "yes." To go against this universal trend of acceptance is to be a party pooper of the first order.

Take that ubiquitous teenage gathering, the "sleepover." I don't think any parent really likes the idea of a teenager heading with pillow and sleeping bag to a stranger's house where the rules are different, the supervision is different, and the temptations are many. Nor do they want an invasion of their own privacy. See, I'm sounding just like a party pooper.

Cherith was the ultimate sleepover advocate. I could never quite put my finger on why I felt uncomfortable with the idea, which made it very difficult to justify saying no. But I would hear little snippets of conversation that gave me cause: *won't be in until late . . .; beer in the frig . . .; boys are coming over . . .; stay up all night . . .; has some cigarettes . . .; she'll never know . . .; stuff from school . . .; don't care . . .; dye her hair . . . ; don't tell parents . . . ; older brother . . .; try it.*

Well, you get the picture. Not all snippets occurred for any one sleepover, but usually there was that underlying sense of unease. I didn't really know what they had planned. Occasionally, Cherith would wear me down, and I would agree.

I always wished I hadn't. One morning Cherith arrived home at six. I never did find out exactly what happened, but as near as I can tell the parents had gone out leaving Cherith and her friends to babysit. From that point on, the story gets hazy. What the parents found when they arrived home (at six o'clock in the morning?) is not clear. Other parents were surprisingly reticent as well to talk about it. Perhaps it's just as well that I don't know.

Sometimes, I'd break down and agree to a sleepover at our house. We had a travel trailer that we used as a guest house at the farm. This was particularly popular for sleepovers since it was completely self-contained and somewhat remote from the main house. One time Cherith had two of her girlfriends staying over and Nathan was bound, on pain of death, to stay away.

Around eight in the evening in a fit of Super-Mom, I headed down to the trailer with some home-made fudge and cocoa. As I opened the door, a thick cloud of cigarette smoke wafted out onto the night air. I knew that one of Cherith's friends smoked, but smoking in the trailer was a "no-no." I felt my anger rise. Three pairs of guilty eyes looked up as I stormed in. Cherith was scrabbling to shove some things into the drawer. I looked closely at the items: a large darning needle, some wads of blood-stained cotton, and a few melting ice cubes. I knew what was going on! Somebody was trying to pierce someone else's ears.

Sure enough, Cherith was the guilty (lucky?) party. I had already said "no" to her pleas for more holes in her ears. One set is enough for now, I told her. When you can afford to get them done yourself, you can go to a jeweler and have them done properly. She had decided to save both time and money.

It wasn't the second set of holes that made me so angry. It was the sneakiness of the counterattack. Coupled with the cigarettes, I had had enough of this particular sleepover. I drove everyone home. The party pooper struck again!

Nathan never liked trucking over to someone else's house to sleep. He wasn't too keen on having someone sharing his room and bed either. Until he was sixteen, I didn't have too many "no's" for Nathan in terms of what everyone else was doing.

Then, someone invented the "field party." A gang of teens would choose a farmer's field (usually belonging to the parents of one of the participants), spread the word, bring their portable boom boxes, refreshments and friends, and have a party. It all sounded so innocent, except that some of the rowdier crowd brought more than sodas to the party. Beer became the drink of choice. Of course, there were no chaperones, no curfews, no rules, no "no's" when it came to a field party.

Nathan desperately wanted to go. I continued to be the party pooper. Nathan claimed that I didn't trust him. That's always the killer line for parents. How do you explain that the teen is right, you don't trust him? You don't trust him to be able to go against the crowd, say no when everyone else is saying yes, refuse when everyone else agrees. You don't think he will be able to handle looking like a "wimp," being accused of being a "wussy" (local term for crybaby), or walking away from his friends. It has nothing to do with the teen's morals, or his upbringing, or even of his intestinal fortitude. It's simply peer pressure, the toughest pressure in the world for a teenager to resist.

I hung in with my "no." When Nathan was eighteen, a new kind of field party, the "Jim Jam," arrived. This party had a live band and attracted teens from far and wide. It was, to my mind, even worse than the original local meetings. Nathan wanted to go. At eighteen, he could have gone with or without my permission and faced the music when he got home. But he asked. Reluctantly, I agreed, laying out the ground rules. No drinking if you're driving the car. Give me a telephone number in case I have to reach you. Get out of there if a fight starts. Leave if there are any drugs.

What made it more difficult was that we were going to an anniversary party for some friends in Montreal, a three-hour drive away. We wouldn't even be home if anything happened.

We got home about two in the morning. On the kitchen counter was a note:

Mom:

I've gone to Jim Jam. I'll be home around 3:30 or so. Please don't worry. I won't drink since I'm driving. I'll be as quiet as possible coming home. Yes, there will be hired cops there, so don't worry. I hope you had a good time at the wedding-thing.

Nate

P.S. Have a good sleep.

The last thing I did was "have a good sleep." Certain words kept going around in my head: "drink, driving, hired cops." At 3:15 I heard Nathan drive in. Well, I thought, at least he's alive, and the car is in one piece.

It's so hard being the party pooper parent. I can remember being so angry at my mother when "everyone else" went to a dance on a school night (the Wednesday night dance was always the best one in town); when "everyone else" went steady at thirteen (Mom made me give Ronnie Bezo back his school sweater); when "everyone else" hung out at the corner store (Mom would come and get me if I wasn't home on time); when "everyone else" dropped out of school at sixteen (Mom told me how much my room-and-board would be if I wasn't at school). Now, I'm doing the same thing to my kids. I know Cherith resented not going to the rock concert in Ottawa on her own (I drove her and asked a younger friend of mine to go with her); not getting a tatoo of a rose on her shoulder (I called the Department of Health and told her the grim facts about tatoo parlors); not wearing the sleazy style of cut up to here and down to there (I once threw out a see-through something she borrowed from a friend).

But, Cherith also went to the next rock concert on her own because she knew what to expect and so did I. She's glad she doesn't have a tatoo and enjoys using the temporary tatoo package I gave to her. And, she's learned how to dress in her own style, which may not be mine, but suits her well.

Nathan couldn't understand why he had to do chores when everyone else was free after school. He resented having to ask for the car or find his own way if the car wasn't available. He got angry when I refused to buy him a motorcycle now so he could pay me back later when he got a job. But he has learned to be responsible for his part of the upkeep of this household. He understands that the car is not his personal property, but is "on loan." He buys his own gas and checks the oil regularly. And he knows

I will help him buy a motorcycle when he has the means to repay the loan.

Whenever I am tempted to give in to avoid a hassle, I need to remind myself that as a Christian, I am not expected to go along with this world. I need to tune myself in to the spirit and listen to the still small voice within that helps me decide when "no" is the Christian response.

Being a party pooper means going against popular opinion. It means a lot more hassles, a lot more arguments, and a lot more teenage resentment and anger. In the long run, it also means teenagers who understand that there are limits in this world.

And Now for the Good News

I have to be careful that I don't say "no" from a holier-than-thou attitude. The "Be Attitude" here is being persecuted (by ticked-off teens perhaps?) because of righteousness. In *Strong's* commentary, *righteousness* can mean correctness of thinking, feeling, and acting. It also means integrity and rightness. I know that if I submit all my decisions to the Lord, pray over each one, then the rightness of the decision is determined by the One who has my life in the palm of His hand. And surely, I can trust God to whisper the right answer.

10.

Great Expectations

Blessed are you when people insult you,
persecute you and falsely say all kinds
of evil against you because of me.
(Matthew 5:11, NIV)

<u>Ten</u>

☺ *Do you remember what it was like the first time you held your little bundle of joy? I do. I knew exactly what this child was going to be like. He was going to be loving, kind, and polite. He would eat anything I placed on the table. He would enjoy wearing the clothes I put out for him each day. And he would never, ever, ever say the "f" word in public!*

I had great expectations.

From the first moment I held him until he was twelve years old, Nathan was what people refer to as "a handful." He demanded, and usually got, every living, breathing second of my attention. He had multiple food allergies. This meant that everything that went into his mouth had to be carefully selected and screened. One wrong bite and I had a screaming, out-of-control, hyperactive child to contend with. Unfortunately, he craved the foods that he couldn't have and hated those I prepared for him. Every mealtime was like manning a battle-front.

His allergies extended to clothing as well. No easy disposable diapers for him: I had the old-fashioned pleasure of cotton washables with no bleach, no fabric-softener, and no super detergents. It seemed that whatever I picked out for him disagreed with his allergy-prone skin. Dressing him was a challenge I hadn't counted on.

As a preacher's kid, he had a lot of expectations to live up to, and he never let anyone down. One Christmas Eve, my mother took him up into the empty balcony of the church for the evening service. Cherith had a cold and wasn't feeling well, and it seemed a good place to keep an eye on both of them. Besides, Nathan was over-the-moon with Christmas excitement (resulting from some pur-loined Christmas candies), and Mom thought this isolation would help calm him down. I was singing in the choir. His daddy was in the pulpit. His granny was busy with his sick sister. Nathan has never liked feeling that he is being ignored. So, he began to lob hymn books down into the congregation below. Little old ladies were screaming and ducking. His daddy yelled at him from the front. I jumped up and headed up the aisle. Nathan had accomplished his purpose.

He may not have exactly said the "f" word in public, but he knew how to get attention anyway.

When Cherith came along, my expectations were a little more realistic. I expected that I would be able to cope with this child more easily than the first. I was right.

But the coping had nothing to do with my newly-acquired child-rearing skills. Cherith was an accommodating child. Until she reached eleven years old, with the exception of a predilection to wander, she was easy to handle.

People were always offering to take Cherith for a weekend, on a trip, to the store, or for a treat. She was a popular choice. No one ever offered to take Nathan anywhere! When I had to go into the hospital for surgery, offers poured in to help with Cherith. In the end, my mother took Nathan home with her—no one else had volunteered.

The trouble is I've always known how my children were going to be. Before they came along, I told everyone else how my children were going to be. I made it quite clear that my little darlings would not have the faults that were so obvious in their little darlings. I let them know that I wouldn't tolerate the kind of behavior that I saw in their children. Frankly, I gave all the parents I knew a pretty hard time about the weaknesses I perceived in their child-rearing skills.

Boy, have I faced a comeuppance! For twelve years, people just had to look at Nathan and know that I didn't have it all together. How many times have I caught a glance between two observers of Nathan's behavior, a glance that said, "I certainly wouldn't allow that kind of thing if he were my child." How many times have I wrestled with Nathan in a shopping mall (where, by the way, he learned that screaming something like, "Please, please Mommy. Don't beat me AGAIN!" was very effective in bringing instant assistance from passers-by) and had to endure the looks of the other shoppers? How many times have I apologized to guests as Nathan continued to holler and yell from his bedroom long after he was "put to bed"?

"You must be firm," people would tell me. How firm can you get? Short of tying him up (which I did do with bed harnesses and walking harnesses), he was impossible to settle down.

"Spare the rod and spoil the child," they'd quote. A smack on the rear had little or no effect. I didn't trust myself to go any further.

"You need to be firm and reason with him." Who were they kidding?

I endured all the overt and covert criticism for years, knowing that my child was a living reminder that I didn't have the parenting stuff down pat. Fortunately, there was always Cherith to show that I could do it.

Then, the wheel turned. I have a theory that at the moment Nathan turned twelve and Cherith turned eleven, they made an agreement. "Okay," said Nathan. "I've kept her busy for the last twelve years. Now, it's your turn." Cheerfully, they reversed their roles.

Nathan was such a "lovely young man." I enjoyed showing him off to my friends—the same friends who had been so critical just a few years earlier.

But Cherith! Her clothes, her language, her friends—all provided endless fodder for those critical voices. I was back in the same defensive mode. Didn't any of the OPPKs have a fault or two? How come the blame for my children's sins of omission and commission was all mine?

Cherith took all the expectations I had for Nathan and used them against me. She suddenly developed all kinds of likes and dislikes when it came to food. Clothes could only be worn if the right label was attached. And . . . yes . . . she did say the "f" word in public! Where did my sweet little girl go? She turned into a teenager.

Then Marnella joined us. Now I had to contend with what other people believed was the "right" way to be a stepmother. Advice poured in from every corner: be tough, be kind, be loving, be impartial, be fair, be honest, be anything but what I already was. They pursed their lips and shook their heads as they perceived my failings in Marnella's attitude, behavior, and habits.

I began to feel that parenting was a life-long sentence to persecution with no chance of parole. At any given moment, one of the darlings under my care was proving to the outside world that I was incompetent. Worse, the outside world felt it was their prerogative to tell me where I was going wrong and criticize me when I continued to go wrong. This wasn't what I had expected when I embarked on this child-rearing business.

It's the expectations that trip me up. I have expectations for my children and the rest of the world has expectations too. When the children don't meet those expectations, I'm the one who takes the blame. How ridiculous!

If I expect it to be sunny tomorrow, and it rains, I don't immediately blame myself. Yet, I have about as much control over many aspects of my children's personalities as I do over the weather. I need to stop taking all the flack. I need to realize that all the persecution, the insults, and the remarks made behind my back are simply false. My children are individual human beings. I cannot mold them like a lump of clay, wonderful as that would be. All I can do is provide a climate in which they can grow and thrive. It's up to the Lord to do the molding.

And Now for the Good News 📖

What a great "Be Attitude" this is—to be free of other people's expectations. I'm also learning to be free from my own expectations as well. I'm learning to love and enjoy the essential person inside those little darlings; to realize that under the mood swings, the outlandish clothing, the silly likes and dislikes, and the nonconformist attitudes lies a child of God.

11.
So, What's Your Point?

Then the king will say to those at his right hand, 'Come, you that are blessed by my Father, inherit the kingdom prepared for you from the foundation of the world.'
(Matthew 25:34)

<u>Eleven</u>

😐 *I'm getting old. I hadn't planned to, but it's happening anyway. When I see mothers with little children, I find it hard to believe that nearly twenty years have passed since I was in their shoes. It literally seems only yesterday that I was the mother struggling with one in the stroller and one on the run. I watch the young mothers wipe up the tears, hand out the ice cream cones, and tie up the shoelaces; and I feel that if I turn around, my two little ones will be right behind me too.*

My friends of those days are now grandparents. Proudly they display photographs, refrigerator art galleries, and the latest bronzed shoe for me to admire. I keep thinking that we're all too young to be dealing with another generation of children.

But we're not. We have gray hair, bifocals, and more than a few bulges where there weren't any twenty years ago. Like it or not, the aging cycle goes on.

I'm not quite at the grandparent stage yet. I'm still reveling in the early empty nest stage. I feel a little like a fledgling myself as I daringly walk through the house wearing nothing but a towel (nobody notices except the dog!). I still find it amazing that milk remains in the refrigerator, towels remain on towel racks, and the car sits in the driveway. It's all very heady stuff after twenty years of living with a two-legged occupation force.

The silence of the house is awesome. No booming stereos, wahwah pedals, or televisions fill the air with their competing sound waves. A visitor once remarked that all the energy goes out of the house when the young people leave. I don't agree: all the noise goes out of the house. Sometimes, I can hear myself think.

That's probably the most profound result of being in an empty nest: I can think. And I've been doing a lot of thinking about my children, their lives, my role, and how it has all moved into another phase. I can't go back and correct any mistakes I perceive in my child-rearing practices, nor can I yet take credit for doing anything right. It's a little like being in a holding pattern of life. Only the next few years will tell whether or not the last few years were successful.

But this empty nest has given me a little perspective on how to use the "Be Attitudes" to cohabit with teenagers. As the kids would say, "So, what's your point?"

When Jesus gave us the Beatitudes, he was really talking about how to "be." He was not telling us to "be" like the rest of the world. In fact, these "Be Attitudes" are diametrically the opposite of how the world expects us to "be."

Jesus tells us that the poor in spirit are blessed. He's talking about humbleness. Yet this world pushes exactly the opposite on our children. They're given the message that they are the most important thing in the world and that the world owes them a living. Just look at the proliferation of child-centered services. Everything from magnificant theme parks (imagine the poor, deprived child who has never visited Disneyland), to specialized restaurants (McDonald's to name one), to designer clothing outlets (OshKosh B'gosh) continually reinforce a child's belief that the world revolves around him or her.

I'm not surprised that my teenagers had such a tough time understanding that the sun did not rise and set on them. I had a hard time believing it too. When I finally broke down and sent Cherith to an expensive riding camp, she felt that she had finally received her just reward. She was furious that I could only afford to send her for one week. For weeks after she returned home, she lay depressed and angry in her room. I felt guilty until I remembered that my "Be Attitude" is to be humble, to accept what the Lord has placed before me. What God had placed before me was finances that did not include expensive camps for the children.

"Blessed are those who mourn," said Jesus. That's not the message we receive from the world. We're told to keep a stiff upper lip, to keep it all inside, and to keep our emotions under wraps. Many kids grow up believing that their parents have no feelings whatsoever. In return, they do not know how to express their own feelings.

I've tried hard to be open about my feelings. There's no doubt that I had no trouble with the yelling and shouting ones, but I've tried to hug and kiss too. Jesus tells us that it's okay to mourn—to show sorrow. That's the emotion most people hide deepest. We need to say when we hurt. Otherwise, our children don't know how to show that they hurt, and they learn to bury it all deeper and deeper. Eventually, they end up doing the same thing with their children, and the cycle of nonfeeling goes on.

One year my teens forgot my birthday. I was hurt and started out with the "stiff upper lip" attitude, pretending that it didn't matter. But it did matter. I realized that it was wrong of me to pretend. So I told them how I felt. They were truly astounded. They hadn't realized that I also wanted to have my birthday noted, just as they expected theirs to be celebrated. More than that, they suddenly realized that I was a human being with feelings.

I hate the saying, "When the going gets tough, the tough get going." Although I'm the first to admit that I like self-help, this goes far beyond that. It implies that there is no power other than what you can provide for yourself. How frightening this must be for our children as they struggle with the world.

Nathan learned early that there is always help when the going gets tough, and that help comes through prayer. He candidly admits that he prayed about his lack of confidence and social skills before he entered into high school. In fact, he was terrified about leaving the familiarity of his junior school and moving on. God answered his prayer, and Nathan is a popular, self-assured young man. The tough don't need to get going; the meek seek God's toughness instead.

This world is a storage house of laid-up treasures. We're continually told that we must have things in order to be okay. It has been hard on my children because we have not been surrounded by a lot of things. At first we couldn't afford them, but even now that God has given me some abundance in my life, I shy away from using it for things. Somehow, I hope that by my example the kids will see that life is rich and full without four cars in the driveway or the latest stereo components in the living room. It's hard for them. All around them they see a world that measures worth by wealth and wealth by possessions. Jesus tells us that in the eyes of the world, we will look poor indeed as we lay up our treasures in heaven, where they may not be decayed or moth-eaten; but they also won't be seen by those who keep a worldly tally.

It's a tough world, the kids are told. You've got to learn how to take care of Number One. Yet, Jesus reminds us to be merciful. Night after night my teens see the television news that shows horrifying accounts of wars, starvation, and violence. There is no evidence of mercy anywhere. Somehow, I have to remind them that Jesus needs his people to bring that mercy to this world. I've tried to do it in little ways. I've encouraged them to make up Christmas baskets for the local food bank; I've let them feel a part of our extended family through the World Vision Fund; I've reminded them of a need to give to the church in both time and money. I don't know if it has made a difference, yet.

How can these same children follow Jesus' admonition to be pure in heart when they are also expected to "be cool"? When she was twelve years old, Cherith took part in a program called V.I.P. ("Very Important Person"). The whole thrust was learning how to say no to peer pressure on smoking, drinking, sex, and drugs. One of their theme songs was "I'd rather be me," which encouraged the kids to follow their own instincts rather than succumb to crowd mentality. The idea was great. The results weren't. Few of her classmates, nor Cherith herself, have resisted the blandishments of this world. It's taken her eight years of her own experimentation to reach a point where she can honestly say, "I'd rather be me." This world is tough on those who try to remain pure in heart.

The peacemakers aren't doing so well either. If you don't stand up and fight, you're a coward, a pushover, or a wimp. This is difficult for boys, particularly, who are continually encouraged to portray a "macho" image. I returned home after one of my speaking trips to find Nathan with his hand in a cast. He had smashed his fist into his locker and broken several knuckles. It turned out that he had been taunted by another boy, and rather than punching him, he hit the locker instead. It wasn't through any desire to be a peacemaker. Nathan realized that he was over eighteen and could be charged with assault, so he chose a nonassaultable object to vent his temper upon.

"Why didn't you just ignore him?" I asked angrily.

"He would have never left me alone," said Nate. "I had to show him what I could do if I wanted to." The peacemakers don't have a chance. Neither do the kids who try to follow a Christian lifestyle. It's all very well knowing that Jesus expects us to be persecuted because of our righteousness, but try telling that to a teenager who is being teased for being different.

In fact, the whole thrust of a teenager's life is to be one of the crowd; to be just like everyone else; and to adopt the dress, habits, and manners of the group. Being different is the kiss of death to teenage popularity.

No wonder I find this whole parenting business confusing. I am also called to be different. The "Be Attitudes" that Jesus requires of me compel me to think, move and act against the flow of this world. The state of "being" that results is different from the state of most of the parents I know.

It's a lonely state. Sometimes I feel as if I am the voice crying in the wilderness, but no one is listening. Sometimes I want to simply give up and say, "Okay, just do what everyone else is doing. It doesn't matter." So far, I haven't given in.

And Now for the Good News

Jesus didn't offer the "Be Attitudes" as casual suggestions for how we should live our lives. He gave them as guidelines for happiness. As a Christian, I may experience a sense of being apart and different from the world that is somewhat disconcerting; but I also experience a happiness that comes from knowing I am living God's plan for me. Sometimes, in the quiet of my empty nest, I fret about the decisions I have made and the ways in which I have tried to guide my teenagers. But I remind myself that as long as those decisions and guidelines have been different from the world, I will be rewarded as Jesus promised me.

Epilogue

This book has been a long time in the writing. Usually, I think about a book for a few months, start jotting down notes, search out some scripture passages, integrate a theme, and then bash out the whole thing in a marathon of writing, rewriting, editing, revising, and praying.

Not this book. I've been dithering with it for over two years. Even as I write this, I'm about 35,000 feet up on a flight from Pittsburgh to Evansville, Indiana; and I'm still dithering. I'm writing this by hand because I didn't bring my laptop computer along.

Why? Because the last few trips I've dragged along the laptop and didn't even opened the darn thing! Each trip I promise myself I'll write a chapter or two, and I never do. I dither instead.

I wonder whether I may have gone to inspiration's well once too often—after all, this is my seventh book. But, I've just finished two secular books for a seminar company, so I know the well isn't dry yet!

I worry that I don't have anything new to say as a Christian. But I continue to present Christian workshops and pinch-hit in local pulpits. My walk with the Lord is still fresh and new.

I fret that people won't be interested in my particular brand of parenting. But people continually ask me to share those experiences, so I know that there must be value in the sharing.

What's the problem? Why am I still dithering?

I'll tell you. I'm not really dithering. I'm *waiting*. Despite all my preaching to the contrary, I kept delaying this book until I could write about my perfect family. I've been *waiting* until that perfect family appeared.

Marnella found a great job. I wrote a page or two. Then, she quit because she didn't like her boss. I didn't write for a month.

Cherith graduated from college. I warmed up the computer. Then, she announced she'd rather go on welfare than work some McJob in a fast-food outlet. I turned off the computer.

Nathan talked about his plans for his career after he graduated from college. I started jotting down some ideas. Then, he rekindled a romance with a neighbor's daughter and mentioned leaving school for marriage. I closed my notebook.

Gerald and I found ourselves alone at last when all three kids moved out (one to an apartment, two to college). I prepared some thoughts on the "empty-nest" syndrome and how to cope. But we loved being alone! We didn't care if they ever came back home! I didn't think such thoughts fit into a Christian book.

And so it went for two years. Only now have I come to realize what my problem was. I didn't want to be anything less than perfect. I wanted you to think that I had it all figured out, that I had faced and triumphed over any difficulties I encountered as the parent of a teenager.

I wanted this book to be a rebuttal to years of reading about all those happy, perfect Christian families who stay together, pray together, and never, ever have an angry word. I wanted to be one of those kinds of families. So, I waited.

How dumb! When I stop and think about people I know who profess to have just such model families, I see all kinds of cracks in their facade. In their eagerness to convince me that their children are all absolutely wonderful, they miss the true joy that comes from the little breakthroughs in family relationships.

Breakthroughs like Marnella handling the sublet of her apartment when Dad refused to bail her out. Or Cherith heading out with a folder of resumes, visiting every store on the main street. Or Nathan making decisions at college that will ensure that he graduates.

Oh, they aren't big things. But in the long run, they're what parenting is all about. The trouble is, these breakthroughs are hard to write about because I have to also write about the negatives that caused these break-through moments. I have to admit that my family is not perfect.

The Christian life isn't a guarantee that it's all going to be perfect. There are bad times, especially with teenagers. However, as a Christian, Rom. 8:28 promises that "all things work together for good."

That's my basic "Be Attitude." Whatever is happening in my life is not my problem. It belongs to God. Only God can see where it fits into the pattern of my life. When I "let go and let God," the results may not look too good on paper, but God can use every aspect that I surrender. By surrendering, I know that God will bring it to perfection according to God's plan.

Many years ago when Gerald was a child, his mother gave him a small New Testament. Inside, she wrote a message in Dutch. I couldn't translate the words, but I could look up the passage that she referenced: "I am confident of this, that the one who began a good work among you will bring it to completion by the day of Jesus Christ" (Phil. 1:6).

The good work in my children has been begun by me. As I love them, discipline them, praise them, pity them, encourage them, guide them, counsel them, teach them, and love them some more, I begin a process that only God can finish.

As I live in the "Be Attitude" of the now, the future is in God's hands.

About the Author

Patricia Wilson lives in Ontario with her husband, Gerald. She is Executive Director of Life Track and travels and speaks extensively at business and personal growth seminars. She is also a freelance writer and has written for such publications as *Women's Circle* in the United States and *The United Church Observer* in Canada. She formerly worked as Director of Marketing and Communications for the St. Lawrence Parks Commission of the Ontario government.

Why Pray When You Can Take Pills and Worry? is her seventh book. Her other books are: *The Daises Are Still Free, Who Put All These Cucumbers in My Garden?, Have You Met My Divine Uncle George?, Too Much Holly, Not Enough Holy?, How Can I Be Over the Hill When I Haven't Seen the Top Yet?,* and *Beyond the Crocodiles.*